Peter Mayall

The development of new chip generations for AI applications on smartphones

bup

Peter Mayall

The development of new chip generations for AI applications on smartphones

ISBN: 978-3-68904-341-4 (Paperback)
ISBN: 978-3-68904-348-3 (e-book)

Copyright: Bremen University Press, Bremen, 2024.
The manuscript may not be used in whole or in part without the prior written consent of the publisher.

First edition
April 2024
Version 1.0
Printed in the European Union
bup@bremenuniversitypress.com
www.bremenuniversitypress.com

Peter Mayall

The development of new chip generations for AI applications on smartphones

Overview

INTRODUCTION	4
THE ROLE OF MODERN CHIPS IN THE DEVELOPMENT OF AI	22
SMARTPHONES AS A PLATFORM FOR AI APPLICATIONS	33
THE BASICS OF AI AND ITS DEPENDENCE ON HARDWARE	41
COMPUTING CAPACITIES FOR AI ALGORITHMS	58
THE EVOLUTION OF MODERN CHIPS FOR AI APPLICATIONS	75
FUTURE TRENDS AND INNOVATIONS	92

Table of contents

INTRODUCTION   4

THE EVOLUTION OF AI TECHNOLOGIES   5
AI: SOFTWARE OR HARDWARE?   8
  SOFTWARE   9
  HARDWARE   17
  INTERACTION BETWEEN SOFTWARE AND HARDWARE   19

THE ROLE OF MODERN CHIPS IN THE DEVELOPMENT OF AI   22

ACCELERATING THE TRAINING OF AI MODELS   22
ENABLING MORE COMPLEX MODELS   24
IMPROVING EFFICIENCY AND REDUCING COSTS   25
PROMOTION OF REAL-TIME APPLICATIONS   27
ADAPTATION TO SPECIFIC REQUIREMENTS   28
THE FUTURE OF AI CHIPS   30

SMARTPHONES AS A PLATFORM FOR AI APPLICATIONS   33

UBIQUITY AND ACCESSIBILITY   33
POWERFUL HARDWARE   33
SENSORS AND DATA COLLECTION   36
IMPROVING THE USER EXPERIENCE   36
PROMOTION OF DEVELOPMENT AND INNOVATION   38

THE BASICS OF AI AND ITS DEPENDENCE ON HARDWARE   41

COMPUTING POWER   41
MEMORY AND MEMORY BANDWIDTH   42
ENERGY EFFICIENCY   44

SPECIALISATION VS. GENERALISATION	45
ACCESSIBILITY	46
BASIC CONCEPTS AND APPLICATIONS OF AI AND ML	47
BASIC CONCEPTS OF AI	47
BASIC CONCEPTS OF MACHINE LEARNING	51

COMPUTING CAPACITIES FOR AI ALGORITHMS — 58

EXTENSIVE DATA RECORDS	58
COMPLEXITY OF THE MODELS	58
REAL-TIME REQUIREMENTS	59
ITERATIVE TRAINING AND OPTIMISATION	59
SPECIALISED HARDWARE	59
TYPES OF CHIPS USED IN AI	60
CPUS (CENTRAL PROCESSING UNITS)	60
USE OF CPUS IN AI	62
GPUS (GRAPHICS PROCESSING UNITS)	63
TPUS (TENSOR PROCESSING UNITS)	67
FPGAS (FIELD-PROGRAMMABLE GATE ARRAYS)	71

THE EVOLUTION OF MODERN CHIPS FOR AI APPLICATIONS — 75

HISTORY OF HARDWARE DEVELOPMENT SPECIFICALLY FOR AI APPLICATIONS.	75
SPECIALISATION AND OPTIMISATION: FROM GPUS TO TPUS AND BEYOND.	78
CASE STUDIES: AI ON SMARTPHONES AND THE ASSOCIATED CHIPS	80
SPECIALISED PROCESSORS	81
DEDICATED AI CHIPS	82
EXAMPLES OF AI CHIPS IN SMARTPHONES	83
APPLE'S NEURAL ENGINE	83
GOOGLE'S TENSOR PROCESSING UNIT (TPU)	85
HUAWEI'S KIRIN CHIPSET WITH NPU	87
SENSORS AND OTHER HARDWARE COMPONENTS	90
OPTIMISATIONS AT SOFTWARE LEVEL	90

FUTURE TRENDS AND INNOVATIONS — 92

FURTHER DEVELOPMENT OF SPECIALISED AI CHIPS	**92**
IMPROVING ENERGY EFFICIENCY	**92**
INTEGRATION OF AI IN ALL ASPECTS OF SMARTPHONE TECHNOLOGY	**93**
EDGE COMPUTING AND THE ROLE OF THE CLOUD	**95**
NEW MATERIALS AND PRODUCTION TECHNIQUES	**97**
CHALLENGES IN THE FURTHER DEVELOPMENT OF AI-ENABLED CHIPS FOR SMARTPHONES	**99**

Introduction

The development of new chip generations specifically for AI applications on smartphones continues to gather pace. These new chips are designed to optimise the performance and efficiency of AI functions on mobile devices. Their design takes into account not only the need to perform complex calculations faster, but also to minimise energy consumption in order to extend battery life. These specialised chips enable a range of advanced features such as enhanced image processing, natural language processing and real-time translation by efficiently processing machine learning and deep neural networks directly on the device.

At the centre of this innovation is both the further development of chip architecture and the use of new materials and production methods. These developments are aimed at creating chips that are not only faster and more powerful, but can also be produced in ever smaller formats to fit into the slim design of modern smartphones. They also help to improve data protection, as more data can be processed directly on the device without having to be transferred to the cloud.

These new chips for AI applications on smartphones symbolise a significant step forward in mobile technology by making it possible to integrate advanced AI functions seamlessly and efficiently into everyday life.

The author works in research and development at a major chip manufacturer.

The evolution of AI technologies

The evolution of artificial intelligence (AI) is a development that has spanned several decades and now impacts almost every aspect of human society. This development has not only changed the way we work, communicate and learn, but also raises fundamental questions about ethics, privacy and the future of human labour.

The beginnings of AI date back to the 1950s, when the term "artificial intelligence" was first coined at the Dartmouth Conference in 1956. During this time, fundamental concepts and algorithms were developed that are still relevant today. This early phase was characterised by great optimism, but researchers soon came up against the limits of computer performance and the algorithms available at the time.

In the decades that followed, AI research experienced ups and downs, often referred to as "AI winters", periods when funding and interest in AI waned due to unmet expectations. Despite these challenges, researchers made important advances in specific areas such as machine translation, speech recognition and expert systems that codify the knowledge of experts in a particular field.

A decisive turning point for AI was the development of more powerful computers and the emergence of the internet, which made it possible to collect and analyse huge amounts of data. This led to the rise of machine learning, in particular deep learning, a technique based on deep neural networks. Neural networks are a core concept of machine learning and artificial intelligence, inspired by the way the human brain works. They consist of a large number of simple, interconnected units, known as artificial neurons, which process data by recognising certain patterns and features in it. The connections between these neurons have weightings that adapt during the learning process in order to perform specific tasks such as image and speech recognition, predictions and decision-making more efficiently.

These methods have made it possible to recognise complex patterns in data and learn to perform tasks such as image and speech recognition with a level of accuracy that was previously not possible.

These advances have accelerated the integration of AI into everyday life, from personal assistants like Siri and Alexa, to the recommendation systems that control the content we watch on platforms like Netflix and YouTube, to more advanced applications like autonomous vehicles and personalised medicine. AI's ability to quickly analyse large amounts of data has also led to breakthroughs in areas such as finance, manufacturing and scientific research.

However, the impact of AI on society is double-edged. While it has the potential to increase productivity, create new products and services and provide solutions to complex problems, there are also significant concerns about the impact on the world of work, privacy and the ethical aspects of automation and surveillance. Increasing automation may lead to significant change in the world of work, with the possibility of many traditional professions disappearing or changing radically.

Similarly, the use of AI in surveillance systems and decision-making raises issues of privacy, bias and transparency. The ability of algorithms to make decisions that can have a major impact on people's lives without the underlying processes being easily understood or scrutinised has led to a debate about the need for ethical guidelines and greater regulation.

It can be said that the evolution of AI technologies has impacted society in transformative ways, opening up new opportunities but also raising new challenges and questions about its application and impact. The future of AI will depend not only on technological advances, but also on how societies address these challenges

The development and integration of artificial intelligence into various aspects of our lives and work harbours enormous potential for transformation. AI systems can often perform tasks faster and more accurately than humans, especially in repetitive or data-intensive tasks, leading to an increase in efficiency and productivity. One of the biggest advantages of AI lies in its ability to analyse large amounts of data, recognise patterns and make informed decisions, which can be applied in areas such as financial analysis, medical diagnostics and climate research.

AI also enables unprecedented personalisation in products and services, from education and medicine to retail, and adapts to the specific needs and preferences of users. In addition, AI is driving the development of new technologies and solutions in various sectors and improving quality of life through automation and intelligent assistance systems that make everyday life easier and provide support for people with disabilities.

AI also plays a crucial role in tackling complex global challenges such as climate change and medical research by developing effective strategies to solve these problems. AI can also expand access to education and knowledge by creating personalised learning environments and overcoming language barriers.

Despite this positive outlook, the introduction of AI requires careful consideration of the associated challenges and ethical considerations. Issues of privacy, job security and the fair use of AI are crucial to ensure that the benefits of AI technology are utilised for the benefit of all and do not lead to new forms of inequality or ethical dilemmas.

AI: software or hardware?

The development and progress of artificial intelligence is an interplay between software and hardware, with each component playing a crucial role. To understand how AI is developed, it is important to consider the functions and contributions of both aspects:

Software

The role of software in the development of artificial intelligence is as central as it is complex.

The software provides the tools and methods with which AI systems are designed, trained, tested and applied. The continuous development of software technologies in AI has made remarkable progress possible in various areas, from automatic speech processing to machine vision and decision-making.

Traditional systems and rule-based approaches

In the early days of artificial intelligence, the development of rule-based systems, also known as expert systems, was at the centre of interest.

These systems aimed to simulate human decision-making processes in specific areas of expertise by basing them on a comprehensive set of rules carefully defined by domain experts. These rules formed the basis for the systems to analyse problems, draw conclusions and make decisions in a similar way to how a human would do it in the respective field.

The main advantage of expert systems was their ability to preserve and make accessible the knowledge and experience of experts in a particular field. They have been used in a variety of fields, from medicine, where they assist with diagnoses, to financial analysis, where they help evaluate investment opportunities. Expert systems have been able to make a valuable contribution in these and other use cases by scaling the expertise of experts and making it usable in situations where human experts may not have been available.

Despite their success, however, rule-based systems quickly reached their limits. Their effectiveness depended heavily on the quality, completeness and timeliness of the rules on which they were based. As these rules were defined by people, they had to be continuously reviewed and updated to keep pace with new findings and changes in their field of application. This necessity made expert systems labour-intensive and expensive to maintain.

Another problem with rule-based systems was their lack of flexibility and adaptability. They were excellent at solving clearly defined problems within their set of rules, but had difficulty dealing with situations that fell outside this framework. This limitation limited their applicability in complex or unpredictable environments where human experts often rely on intuition and experience to make decisions.

With the advent of machine learning and deep learning, the boundaries of AI have expanded considerably. These newer approaches allow systems to learn and generalise from data rather than being based on predefined rules. This allows AI systems to react more flexibly to a wider range of problems and adapt better to changes and new information. Nevertheless, rule-based systems remain valuable in certain contexts, especially where clear, well-defined rules exist and where transparency and traceability of decision-making are crucial.

Machine learning and neural networks

The development and spread of machine learning has fundamentally changed and expanded the landscape of artificial intelligence.

While rule-based systems are based on a fixed set of rules defined by humans, machine learning models are based on the ability to learn independently from data. These models identify patterns and relationships within large data sets and improve their performance over time through experience, without the need for explicit instructions or rules to be programmed.

- Adaptability and flexibility: One of the biggest advantages of machine learning is its adaptability. Machine learning models can perform tasks and solve problems for which they were not explicitly programmed. This ability allows AI systems to dynamically adapt to new data and changing environments, making them particularly valuable for applications where change and unpredictability are the norm.
- Data analysis and pattern recognition: Machine learning is particularly powerful in analysing data and recognising complex patterns that are not visible to the human eye. This is used in a variety of fields, from medical diagnostics, where

machine learning can help recognise diseases based on subtle signs in imaging data, to the financial world, where it can identify patterns in market data that indicate future trends.
- Personalisation: Another area where machine learning is having a significant impact is personalisation. Whether it's adapting advertising content, curating news feeds on social media or recommending products in online retail, machine learning enables a high degree of personalisation by learning and predicting individual preferences and behavioural patterns from data.
- Automation: Machine learning is also driving automation by taking over routine tasks and supporting decision-making processes in areas such as customer service, supply chain management and even automated vehicle guidance. This automation can lead to significant efficiency gains and allow humans to focus on more complex and creative tasks.

The quality of the predictions or decisions made by machine learning models depends heavily on the quality and variety of the training data used. Bias in the data can lead to distorted or unfair results, which emphasises the need to place ethical considerations at the centre of the development of AI systems.

The revolution triggered by machine learning in the AI landscape is. As we continue to explore and realise the potential of this technology, it is crucial to carefully navigate the associated challenges and ethical issues to ensure that the benefits of AI are harnessed for the benefit of all.

Deep learning

Deep learning, a specialised and advanced form of machine learning, has revolutionised the way machines understand and interpret data. By using deep neural networks, which consist of many processing layers, deep learning can recognise complex patterns in large data sets. This ability to learn and generalise from data has led to breakthroughs in many areas and enabled applications that were considered futuristic just a few years ago.

- Image recognition: One of the most striking examples of the power of deep learning is image recognition. Modern AI systems can analyse images with an accuracy that is often comparable to human perception. This is used in a wide range of applications, from automatic tagging in social media to diagnostic support in medical imaging and object recognition in autonomous vehicles.
- Speech recognition and processing: Deep learning has also enabled significant advances in speech recognition and processing. Voice assistants such as Siri, Google Assistant and Alexa are based on deep learning models that enable them to understand spoken requests and respond in natural language. This technology also supports

the development of real-time translation systems and improved communication aids for people with speech disabilities.
- Natural language processing (NLP): Beyond pure speech recognition, deep learning has dramatically improved the ability of computers to recognise and respond to the meaning of text. From chatbots that can hold realistic conversations to systems that analyse and summarise complex documents, NLP has transformed human-machine interaction.
- Reinforced learning and decision making: Deep learning is also driving developments in the field of reinforcement learning, where AI systems learn from their environment through rewards and optimise their strategies to achieve goals. This has led to impressive demonstrations in games such as Go and chess, where AI systems have defeated human champions, but also has practical applications in robotics and automated system control.

Despite this impressive progress, deep learning also brings challenges. The technology requires large amounts of training data and significant computing power, which raises issues of sustainability and access. Furthermore, when trained with biased data, deep learning models can reproduce these biases in their predictions and decisions, emphasising the need for careful review and adjustment of the training data.

Software tools and libraries

The development and rapid progress in artificial intelligence is closely linked to the emergence and further development of specialised software tools and libraries. These tools form the backbone of modern AI research and application by providing complex algorithms and data structures required for machine learning and deep learning. Among the most prominent are TensorFlow, PyTorch and Keras, each with their own strengths and communities.

- TensorFlow, developed by Google, is one of the most widely used libraries for machine learning. It provides a comprehensive and flexible platform for the design, training and deployment of AI models and is used in both research and industry for a variety of applications. TensorFlow is characterised by its scalability, allowing models to be efficiently trained from single CPUs to large clusters of GPUs and TPUs.
- PyTorch, originally developed by Facebook, has gained a strong following due to its ease of use and flexibility, especially in the development of deep learning models. PyTorch provides a dynamic computational graph system that allows developers to make changes to the architecture and algorithms in real time, facilitating experimentation and prototyping.
- Keras is another popular high-level neural networks API that was originally started as an

independent project and is now tightly integrated with TensorFlow. Keras is characterised by its simplicity and ease of use, which makes it particularly attractive for beginners in the field of machine learning. It enables quick and easy prototyping and supports both convolutional networks and recurrent networks.

These tools and libraries are constantly under development with the aim of increasing efficiency, facilitating access and enabling the creation of more complex and powerful AI systems. The communities behind these projects play a crucial role by making ongoing contributions, from fixing bugs to developing new features and improvements. This collective approach helps ensure that the tools can keep pace with the rapidly evolving needs of AI research and application.

In addition, the availability of extensive data sets and the improvement of hardware capacities, in particular the availability of powerful GPUs, have further accelerated the development and training of sophisticated AI models. The combination of advanced software tools, extensive data and powerful hardware forms the foundation for current and future successes in the field of artificial intelligence. The accessibility of these resources is increasingly democratising AI research and development, opening the door to innovation on a broad scale with the potential to transform almost every aspect of society.

The dynamics in software development for AI reflect the rapid progress and broad application possibilities of artificial intelligence. With every advance in software technology, the boundaries of what is possible with AI are expanding, opening up new ways of solving complex problems and developing innovative solutions in various areas.

Hardware

Hardware plays just as decisive a role in the evolution and application of artificial intelligence as software.

The specific computing power and memory requirements of AI models have led to the development of specialised hardware designed to maximise the efficiency and effectiveness of AI applications.

GPUs and their role in AI

Graphics processing units (GPUs) were one of the first hardware innovations to accelerate AI research and development.

Originally designed for processing graphics applications, it turned out that GPUs can also perform parallel calculations very efficiently, making them ideal for training AI models. Due to their ability to process thousands of threads simultaneously, GPUs can perform complex mathematical calculations required for the training of neural networks much faster than conventional CPUs.

TPUs and their specialisation in AI

Tensor Processing Units (TPUs) are another significant innovation in AI hardware. Developed by Google specifically for deep learning tasks, TPUs are optimised to efficiently process the specific computations used in neural networks. TPUs offer even greater efficiency in the training and inference of AI models, especially for applications that require high computing power, such as speech and image recognition.

FPGAs and their flexibility

Field-Programmable Gate Arrays (FPGAs) offer a flexible hardware solution that can be programmed for specific applications, including AI. Their reconfigurability makes FPGAs particularly valuable for customised AI applications and for situations where the hardware needs to be adapted to new algorithms or models. Although they do not always offer the same raw performance as GPUs or TPUs, their customisability allows them to be used in diverse and rapidly evolving AI applications.

Importance of hardware development

The development of AI-specific hardware is crucial to pushing the boundaries of what is possible with AI. With each generation of hardware, the speed, energy efficiency and capacity to train and execute complex AI models improves. These advances allow researchers and developers to create more innovative and powerful AI applications that were previously impossible due to hardware limitations.

In the future, hardware development will continue to play a key role by forming the basis for the next generation of AI systems. Research will focus not only on increasing computing power, but also on reducing energy consumption and minimising latency to increase the efficiency and accessibility of AI technologies for a wider range of applications and users.

Interaction of software and hardware

The symbiosis between software and hardware is the foundation on which the progress of artificial intelligence rests. This dynamic interaction not only determines the limits of what is currently possible, but also drives innovation and breakthroughs in AI research and application.

Hardware innovation driven by software

Developments in AI software, such as advanced algorithms and machine learning models, are constantly placing new demands on computing power and efficiency. For example, deep learning models, especially those that are trained on very large data sets, require enormous amounts of computing power and memory. The limits of existing hardware therefore pose a direct challenge for the realisation and scaling of such models.

This in turn stimulates the development of new hardware solutions specifically designed for the requirements of AI software, such as GPUs, TPUs and FPGAs, which enable more efficient calculations and thus make the realisation of more complex AI projects feasible.

Hardware innovations inspire software development

On the other hand, advances in hardware open up new possibilities for software development. By increasing the available computing power and efficiency, software developers can design more complex models and algorithms that were previously impossible to realise. This leads to qualitative leaps in the performance of AI applications, for example in the accuracy of speech and image recognition systems. The availability of more powerful and specialised hardware also encourages researchers to pursue innovative approaches in AI research that go beyond traditional methods.

The need for harmonisation

Optimal coordination between software and hardware is crucial to maximise the efficiency and performance of AI systems.

Developers must consider not only the specific capabilities and limitations of the available hardware, but also how their software designs utilise it. Conversely, hardware engineers need to understand what current and future AI models require of the computing architecture in order to design devices that effectively fulfil these needs.

Future-orientated development

The ongoing evolution of both AI software and hardware requires forward-looking planning and collaboration between the areas. Research and development efforts must not only consider current requirements, but also anticipate how AI technologies might evolve. This includes working on new architectures that offer even greater computing power and efficiency, as well as developing software frameworks that can take full advantage of these advances.

Overall, the interaction between AI software and hardware is a key driver of progress in artificial intelligence. The ability to harmoniously integrate and continuously develop these two components will continue to be crucial in order to push the boundaries of what is possible in AI and find innovative solutions to complex challenges.

In practice, this means that advances in AI are not achieved in isolation by software or hardware alone. Rather, it is a synergistic development in which improvements in software technology define the requirements for hardware and innovations in hardware open up new possibilities for software research and application.

The role of modern chips in the development of AI

Modern chips play a central role in the development and use of artificial intelligence. These specialised processors, including graphics processing units (GPUs), tensor processing units (TPUs) and field-programmable gate arrays (FPGAs), are critical to advances in AI by providing the computing power and efficiency needed to train and execute complex algorithms and models. The role of these modern chips can be concretised in several key areas:

Accelerating the training of AI models

The training of AI models, especially deep learning models, actually places immense demands on computing power, as it involves the optimisation of millions or even billions of parameters. This challenge has led to the development and use of specialised hardware capable of efficiently performing the massive parallel computations required. GPUs (Graphics Processing Units) and TPUs (Tensor Processing Units) are examples of such specialised chips that play a crucial role in accelerating the training process.

GPUs were originally developed for graphics and video processing tasks, but their ability to perform parallel computations makes them ideal for training AI models.

Compared to CPUs, which have a limited number of cores and perform tasks sequentially, GPUs have hundreds or thousands of smaller cores that allow them to perform many calculations simultaneously. This feature is particularly advantageous for training deep learning models, where a large number of operations need to be performed on the data simultaneously.

TPUs, developed by Google, are even more specifically geared towards AI tasks. They are specially optimised to perform the tensor operations typical of deep learning with high efficiency. TPUs offer even greater specialisation than GPUs and are able to perform the training and inference of AI models with impressive speed and energy efficiency. Due to their architecture, TPUs can process large amounts of matrix multiplications and other tensor operations that are common in deep learning very efficiently.

The use of GPUs and TPUs has dramatically improved the feasibility and speed of training AI models. While training complex models on CPUs can take days or even weeks, GPUs and TPUs allow this process to be significantly accelerated, often to hours or days. This acceleration is crucial for research and development in AI, as it allows experiments to be conducted faster, models to be iteratively improved and new architectures and algorithms to be explored in a fraction of the time previously required.

In addition, the availability of these powerful computing resources has driven the accessibility and democratisation of AI research. Cloud-based services provide access to GPUs and TPUs for researchers and developers around the world, lowering the barriers to entry into AI research and encouraging wider participation and innovation.

Enabling more complex models

The increased computing power provided by modern chips such as GPUs and TPUs has a transformative effect on the field of artificial intelligence.

These specialised processors enable the development of more complex and in-depth AI models that are able to recognise finer patterns in data and make more precise predictions or analyses. The importance of these technological advances can be seen particularly well in breakthroughs in areas such as speech processing and image recognition.

The emergence of sophisticated language models that can generate human-like texts, answer complex questions and communicate in natural language is based on the ability to process and learn from huge data sets. This would not be possible without the parallel processing capacity and speed offered by modern chips. Similarly, in image recognition, deep learning models have significantly improved the accuracy and ability to interpret images, ranging from medical diagnostics to autonomous vehicle navigation. The computing power behind this makes it possible to quickly analyse millions of images to train models that are then able to handle complex visual tasks.

While the power of modern chips has enabled many of today's breakthroughs in AI, it also comes with the need to develop more efficient algorithms and minimise energy consumption. Balancing the computing power required for advanced AI models with the sustainability of these processes is an ongoing challenge.

The future of AI will depend heavily on further improvements in hardware technology. Research into new chip architectures and energy-saving technologies is crucial to enable the next wave of AI innovation while minimising environmental impact. Collaboration between the fields of hardware development and AI research remains a key driver of progress that has the potential to transform almost every aspect of our lives.

Improving efficiency and reducing costs

Modern chips, often referred to as AI accelerators, are specifically designed to make the extensive and complex calculations required for the training and operation of AI models more efficient. Optimisation for these specific tasks enables a sustainable increase in the speed of AI training and inference processes, which in turn shortens the development cycles of AI-based solutions.

A key feature of these chips is their ability to save energy. By performing calculations faster and with lower energy consumption, they help to reduce the operating costs of AI systems. This efficiency gain is particularly important as the training of AI models, especially deep neural networks, is enormously computationally intensive and can consume significant amounts of electrical energy. By reducing energy requirements, AI technologies not only become more environmentally friendly, but also more economically attractive.

In addition, advances in chip technology are having a democratising effect on AI research and development. By lowering the cost of training and operating AI systems, they open the door to a wider range of players. Research organisations, companies and developers with different budgets will be able to access and use high-quality AI technologies. This is an important step towards increasing innovation and promoting the use of AI in various areas.

Another aspect supported by the specialised chips is the ability to develop customised solutions. By customising the hardware to specific AI tasks, developers and researchers can create AI models that are tailored to the unique requirements of their projects or products. This leads to improved performance and efficiency that might not be achievable with more generalised computing resources.

Promotion of real-time applications

The ability to make decisions in real time is a key aspect of many modern AI applications and is driving the need for specialised hardware.

In areas such as autonomous vehicles, real-time language translation and interactive AI systems, fast processing and analysis of data is not only desirable, but absolutely critical for the functionality and safety of the technology. The development of modern chips that are tailored to these requirements therefore plays a key role in the realisation of such advanced AI applications.

Autonomous vehicles, for example, must be able to interpret their surroundings in milliseconds in order to make decisions about navigation, speed adjustments and evasive manoeuvres. The complexity of the data to be processed, from camera images to radar and lidar signals, requires enormous computing power. Modern chips make it possible to analyse and implement this data in real time by being specially optimised for the parallel processing of large volumes of data. This capability is crucial to ensure the safety and efficiency of autonomous vehicles.

In real-time language translation, modern chips make it possible to translate spoken language into another language almost instantaneously. This requires not only fast processing of acoustic signals, but also analysing them using complex language models in order to correctly capture the context and meaning. The efficiency of modern chips in processing these tasks makes it possible to overcome language barriers in real time, simplifying communication in a globalised world.

Interactive AI systems, such as those used in virtual assistants or interactive entertainment experiences, also benefit from fast data processing. The ability to immediately process and respond to user input makes interaction with such systems natural and intuitive. Modern chips help to ensure that these systems are not only fast, but also able to use complex language models or behavioural patterns in real time to generate relevant and contextual responses.

Specialised chips are therefore more than just a technical achievement; they are enablers for a variety of applications that make our lives safer, easier and more connected. Their ability to process data efficiently in real time makes them indispensable for the implementation and smooth operation of technologies that rely on fast decision-making. These chips are an essential building block in the infrastructure of modern AI applications, enabling innovative solutions and driving technological progress.

Customisation to specific requirements

The flexibility and customisability of modern chips such as field-programmable gate arrays (FPGAs) represent a significant advance in the world of hardware, particularly in the context of AI applications. FPGAs are designed so that they can be programmed for specific applications or tasks by the end user or developer after manufacture. This feature distinguishes them from conventional processors and specialised AI chips, which have a fixed architecture and functionality. The ability to customise the hardware to specific needs makes FPGAs a powerful tool for the development and implementation of AI applications.

A key advantage of FPGAs is their ability to be optimised for a variety of AI tasks, including but not limited to image and speech processing, pattern recognition and data analysis. Unlike traditional CPUs (Central Processing Units) and GPUs (Graphics Processing Units), which are geared towards broader application areas, FPGAs can be configured to optimally support the specific computational patterns and efficiencies required for a particular AI application. This can lead to significantly higher performance and energy efficiency, especially in scenarios where real-time processing and fast data analyses are crucial.

The configurability of FPGAs also offers remarkable flexibility in terms of updating and customising AI systems. Developers can change the logic of FPGA chips to implement new algorithms or optimise the performance of existing applications without having to replace the physical hardware. This adaptability is particularly valuable in a field that is evolving as rapidly as AI, as it allows developers to keep pace with new research findings or requirements without having to make significant investments in new hardware.

In addition, FPGAs offer a solution for implementing AI applications in environments where power consumption is a critical factor. By optimising the hardware for specific tasks, FPGAs can operate more efficiently than general processors, making them ideal for use in mobile devices, embedded systems and other scenarios where energy efficiency is paramount.

The future of AI chips

Continuous development and innovation in the field of AI chips are fundamental drivers that are shaping the future of artificial intelligence.

This dynamic is of key importance, as the demands on AI systems are constantly increasing in terms of both computing power and efficiency. Research groups and companies worldwide are involved in an ongoing race to develop the next generation of processors that exceed the performance limits of existing technologies. The goal is to create chips that are faster, more energy efficient and offer specialised functions for novel AI applications. These endeavours are not only technological challenges, but also essential to fully exploit the potential of AI and open up new fields of application.

One of the main focal points is the acceleration of AI calculations. As AI models become increasingly complex, especially in the field of machine learning and deep neural networks, they require significant computing power. The development of chips that can perform these calculations faster is crucial to reduce training times and enable real-time inference. This has a direct impact on the efficiency and applicability of AI in the real world, from natural language processing to visual recognition.

Energy efficiency is another critical area. As AI applications are increasingly used in mobile devices and at the edge (i.e. directly at the data source), it is important to minimise energy consumption in order to extend battery life and improve sustainability. Advances in chip technology that lead to greater energy efficiency are therefore of great importance. This includes not only the optimisation of hardware for specific AI calculations, but also the development of new architectures that minimise energy consumption and heat generation.

In addition, emerging AI applications require specialised functions that cannot be handled efficiently by generic processors. This has led to the development of customised chips, such as FPGAs for flexible configurations or ASICs (Application-Specific Integrated Circuits) for highly specialised tasks. This specialisation makes it possible to develop tailor-made solutions for specific challenges, from improving speech recognition to accelerating genome sequencing.

The effects of these technological advances are far-reaching and extend across numerous fields. In science, for example, more powerful AI chips make it possible to analyse larger amounts of data in less time, which accelerates new findings in research. In medicine, improved AI systems can contribute to the early detection of diseases, enable more personalised treatment plans and make surgical procedures more precise. In the entertainment industry, advanced AI chips open up new possibilities for immersive experiences, from highly realistic games to personalised content.

The future of AI is therefore inextricably linked to the development of new chip technologies. This continuous innovation is the key to pushing the boundaries of what is possible with AI and opening up new application possibilities. By improving the performance, efficiency and specialisation of AI chips, it will be possible to overcome the challenges of today and realise the visions of tomorrow.

Smartphones as a platform for AI applications

In recent years, smartphones have developed into a central platform for the application and dissemination of artificial intelligence.

These devices have become ubiquitous in our everyday lives and offer a unique foundation for AI-based applications thanks to their advanced capabilities and broad user base. The importance of smartphones as a platform for AI can be illustrated by several key aspects.

Ubiquity and accessibility

Smartphones are widely used around the world and therefore offer a far-reaching platform for AI applications. They enable millions of people to benefit from advances in AI, regardless of their location or access to traditional computing technology. This ubiquity makes smartphones a powerful tool for bringing AI services to a wide audience.

Powerful hardware

The rapid development of smartphone hardware has led to a remarkable improvement in the capabilities of these devices, particularly in the field of artificial intelligence.

Modern smartphones are equipped with advanced processors and graphics units that are specially optimised for the efficient execution of AI algorithms. These hardware improvements mark a significant advance in mobile technology, enabling the processing of complex AI-based tasks directly on the device - a concept often referred to as edge computing. Independence from cloud-based servers for certain tasks brings benefits including improved privacy, lower latency and reduced reliance on continuous internet connections.

Functions such as real-time language translation, image recognition and augmented reality are practical examples of applications that benefit significantly from these developments. By utilising AI technologies directly on the device, these functions can be performed in real time and with impressive accuracy, significantly improving the user experience.

Real-time language translation, for example, was once (and often still is) a task that required powerful servers in the cloud. However, the optimisation of smartphone hardware for AI algorithms has made it possible to process and translate voice signals in real time, without noticeable delays. These improvements not only support more natural communication across language barriers, but also make the technology accessible in environments without a stable internet connection.

Image recognition on smartphones has also benefited from specialised AI chips. Applications that recognise and interpret objects, faces or even text in images now run faster and more efficiently, enabling numerous applications from photography to navigation and security.

Processing these tasks locally not only reduces latency, but also improves security and privacy as sensitive data does not have to leave the device.

Augmented reality (AR) is another field that has received a significant boost thanks to AI optimisation in smartphone hardware. This is a technology that embeds digital information such as images, videos and 3D models into the real world. This digital content is superimposed directly over what we see around us, creating an augmented reality in which virtual and physical objects coexist. AR differs from virtual reality (VR) in that it does not replace the real world, but complements it. Users can continue to perceive the real environment through AR, enriched with additional digital elements.

This technology is implemented in real time and interactively, which means that the digital overlays can adapt dynamically to changes in the real environment or in the user's perspective. A classic example of this is the mobile game Pokémon Go, in which players search for and capture virtual creatures in their real environment. However, the applications of AR are much broader and range from education, where it is used to illustrate complex scientific concepts, for example, to retail, which allows customers to try on products virtually or project them into their living spaces, to industry, where AR is used for maintenance and repair instructions.

Interaction with AR typically takes place via devices that have a camera and a display, such as smartphones, tablets or specialised AR glasses. The device's camera captures the real world, while the AR software overlays the digital content based on image analysis and device orientation. The ongoing development of smartphone hardware, in particular more powerful processors and improved sensors, has helped to make AR accessible to a wider audience and integrate the technology into a variety of everyday applications.

AR applications require fast analysis and interpretation of the real world in order to seamlessly integrate digital information or objects. The performance of modern smartphone chips makes it possible to perform these complex calculations in real time, resulting in smoother and more immersive AR experiences.

Sensors and data collection

Smartphones are equipped with a variety of sensors, including cameras, microphones, gyroscopes and GPS. These sensors continuously collect data that can be used for AI applications to provide personalised and contextual services. For example, AI algorithms can use the information collected by the sensors to understand user behaviour, provide personalised recommendations or interpret the user's environment.

Improving the user experience

Artificial intelligence has become an integral part of modern smartphones and contributes significantly to improving the user experience.

By integrating AI technologies into smartphones, these devices can now perform a variety of tasks more intelligently, efficiently and in a more user-friendly way. AI enables smartphones to learn from interactions with the user, adapt and predict what the user might need next, resulting in a personalised and intuitive user experience.

One of the most striking examples of the use of AI on smartphones are intelligent personal assistants. These assistants, such as Siri, Google Assistant or Bixby, use advanced voice processing technologies to understand natural language and respond to voice commands. They can answer questions, set reminders, control the smart home and even perform more complex tasks such as booking reservations. These assistants are constantly learning and improving with every interaction to provide even more relevant and personalised answers.

In the field of photography, the integration of AI has also brought revolutionary improvements. Modern smartphones use AI-based image recognition technologies to identify scenes and objects in photos and automatically adjust camera settings to get the best possible shots. This technology can also be used to enhance images after they have been taken, for example by removing blur, adjusting the exposure or adding bokeh effects for portrait shots. In addition, AI algorithms enable innovative functions such as recognising faces and smiles to automatically capture the perfect moment for a photo.

Another area in which AI is transforming the use of smartphones is battery management. By learning the user's usage patterns, AI can control adaptive battery management systems that optimise energy efficiency. These systems intelligently adjust the performance of the device and the energy consumption of the apps to maximise battery life. For example, they can recognise when certain apps are typically used and adjust resource allocation accordingly or reduce unnecessary background activity if the phone is rarely used.

These examples illustrate how AI has fundamentally improved interaction with smartphones. By learning from users' behaviour and adapting to their preferences, AI technologies offer a personalised experience that goes far beyond the capabilities of traditional, non-learning systems. The ongoing integration of AI into smartphones promises to further refine and enrich the way we interact with our devices by making them even smarter, more useful and more intuitive.

Promotion of development and innovation

The rapid spread of smartphones and the progressive integration of artificial intelligence (AI) into these devices have created a fertile ecosystem for developers and companies that is fuelling innovation on an unprecedented scale.

This dynamic environment has transformed the app market and led to a major growth in AI-based applications that offer customised services in a variety of areas. The unique combination of ubiquitous smartphone usage and advanced AI technologies opens up new opportunities for the development and delivery of applications that simplify, enrich and improve daily life.

In healthcare, for example, AI-based apps are enabling users to better monitor and manage their health. From apps that detect skin conditions through image analysis to those that use data analytics to create personalised fitness and nutrition plans, AI is changing the way we think and act about health and wellness. These technologies can also be used to support remote patient monitoring and predict health risks, which is particularly valuable in rural or underserved areas.

In the education sector, AI-based apps offer personalised learning experiences by analysing the progress and preferences of learners and then providing tailored content and exercises. This ranges from language learning applications that provide personalised feedback to platforms that teach complex scientific concepts through interactive simulations. The ability to tailor learning content to the needs of each individual has the potential to make education more accessible and effective.

In the financial sector, AI-based apps are revolutionising the way we think about money management and investments. Applications that analyse user behaviour to provide personalised savings tips or those that perform complex market analysis to make investment recommendations are becoming increasingly popular. These technologies are helping to make financial services more democratic by making professional advice and advanced analytical tools accessible to a wider section of the population.

AI-based apps are also driving innovation in the entertainment sector. From personalised music and video streaming services that make recommendations based on previous consumption behaviour to games that adapt to the user's playing style, these applications offer a personalised experience.

This development environment not only promotes the continuous innovation and growth of AI applications designed specifically for mobile devices, but also encourages constant reflection and improvement of the underlying AI technologies. The proximity to the end user and the direct feedback that developers receive via app stores accelerate the innovation cycle and enable rapid adaptation and optimisation of applications. The integration of AI in smartphones is therefore not only a catalyst for technological innovation, but also a driver of social and economic change by making powerful, personalised and intuitive services accessible to a broad user base.

To summarise, smartphones play a key role in the spread and application of AI. They offer an accessible, powerful and personalised platform that has the potential to integrate AI technologies into the daily lives of billions of people worldwide.

The basics of AI and its dependence on hardware

The foundations of artificial intelligence encompass a wide range of technologies, methods and principles that aim to enable machines to perform tasks that require human intelligence.

This includes understanding, learning, planning, speech recognition and problem solving.

The ability of AI systems to learn from experience, recognise patterns in data and make decisions based on these findings is central to the development of intelligent applications. However, the implementation and effectiveness of these systems are increasingly dependent on the underlying hardware. This dependency manifests itself in several key areas:

Computing power

The development and training of AI models, especially in areas such as machine learning and deep learning, are computationally intensive processes. They require a significant amount of computing power to adjust millions or even billions of parameters used in the models. Modern processors such as GPUs (Graphics Processing Units), TPUs (Tensor Processing Units) and specialised AI chips provide the high computing power needed for these tasks by enabling parallel processing and efficient matrix operations that are critical for training AI models.

Memory and memory bandwidth

The effectiveness of artificial intelligence and machine learning depends to a large extent on the ability to process and analyse large amounts of data quickly and efficiently. The computing power of the processors is a critical factor here, but it is only one part of the equation. At least as important are sufficient memory and high memory bandwidth, which are crucial to maximise the efficiency of the training process and the execution of AI models. Taken together, these factors define the performance of AI systems.

Memory plays an equally important role, as it holds the data that is processed by the processors. If there is insufficient memory, data must be processed in smaller batches or reloaded from slower storage media, which can slow down the process. Memory capacity must be large enough to hold the enormous amounts of data required to train AI models, especially deep neural networks that are trained on large data sets.

Memory bandwidth - the speed at which data can be moved between the memory and the processors - is another crucial factor. High memory bandwidths allow data to be delivered to the processors fast enough to ensure continuous, efficient processing. Limited bandwidth, on the other hand, can lead to bottlenecks that slow down the entire process as processors have to wait for access to data.

High Bandwidth Memory (HBM) represents a significant advancement in memory technology, specifically designed to meet the high demands of modern AI systems. At its core, HBM addresses the problem of memory bandwidth, which often limits traditional memory solutions such as DDR (Double Data Rate) memory in terms of the speed at which data can be transferred between the memory and the processor units.

HBM achieves its high bandwidth through a radically different architecture compared to traditional memory designs. Instead of relying on a wide interface with a high clock rate, HBM utilises a much larger number of data channels, each operating at a lower clock rate. This design allows HBM to move data much faster, resulting in a significant increase in overall bandwidth. In addition, HBM is physically placed closer to the processor or GPU, often right next to the chip or even stacked and connected by silicon interposers. This physical proximity further reduces data transfer latency and improves system efficiency.

The benefits of HBM are particularly noticeable in applications that require intensive data processing, as is the case with AI and machine learning. AI models, especially deep neural networks, benefit from the ability to move large data sets and models through memory faster, reducing training times and increasing inference speed. This is crucial for applications that need to work in real-time or near real-time, such as autonomous driving, real-time translation services or interactive AI assistants.

HBM also supports the development of more complex and powerful AI models, as developers are no longer limited to the same extent by memory bandwidth. This opens up new possibilities for research and development in AI, as models can be made deeper, more precise and therefore more powerful without having to accept disproportionate losses in execution speed.

The balance between processor performance, memory capacity and memory bandwidth is now crucial for the optimisation of AI systems.

Energy efficiency

Energy efficiency, as described above, is a key factor in AI hardware, especially for applications running on mobile devices or in large-scale data centres. Energy-efficient hardware reduces power consumption and associated costs, which is particularly important as training AI models and running AI applications can be energy-intensive. Specialised AI chips and processors are often designed to offer higher energy efficiency compared to general processors.

Specialisation vs. generalisation

The distinction between general CPUs and specialised AI hardware components such as GPUs (Graphics Processing Units) and TPUs (Tensor Processing Units) is fundamental when it comes to running AI applications. CPUs, the centrepieces of most computers, are designed for a wide range of tasks. They can handle everything from simple computational tasks to complex logical operations. Their architecture is designed for flexibility and the ability to process data sequentially, making them ideal for general computing tasks.

In contrast, GPUs were originally developed for processing graphics and images, but their ability to perform many calculations in parallel makes them particularly valuable for AI applications as well. GPUs can run thousands of threads simultaneously, making them ideal for the massive parallel computing operations common in machine learning and deep learning. This parallel processing capability means that GPUs can train and execute AI models and algorithms much faster than CPUs.

TPUs are even more specific to AI tasks and have been designed from the ground up to efficiently support machine learning. TPUs optimise certain mathematical operations that frequently occur in AI calculations, such as matrix multiplication, which can lead to even faster calculations compared to GPUs. Google, for example, uses TPUs internally to train and run its AI models, resulting in significant performance improvements.

The choice between CPUs, GPUs and TPUs strongly depends on the specific AI application. While CPUs are still essential due to their flexibility and ability to handle a wide range of tasks, GPUs and TPUs offer key advantages for AI computations. The decision on which hardware to use is based on a number of factors, including the nature of the AI task, the size and complexity of the model, time and cost constraints, and the specific requirements of the application.

The specialisation of GPUs and TPUs makes it possible to perform AI computations more efficiently and faster, but this specialisation comes with the trade-off of flexibility. GPUs and TPUs are optimised for certain types of computations and may not be as effective at tasks outside of these specialisations. In some cases, especially for smaller or less computationally intensive AI projects, a CPU might be sufficient and a more cost-effective option. However, for large-scale AI projects that require intensive computation, the benefits of specialised hardware clearly outweigh the potential limitations in flexibility.

Accessibility

The availability and accessibility of AI-friendly hardware determines who is able to develop and train AI models. While large companies and research organisations may have access to the latest technologies, it is important that the development tools and hardware are also accessible to smaller development teams and individuals to support a wide range of innovations and applications.

Overall, the development of AI is inextricably linked to the evolution of hardware. While the software defines the "intelligence" of AI systems, it is the hardware that makes this intelligence realisable and practical. The future of AI therefore depends not only on breakthroughs in algorithms and data science, but also on advances in the hardware that supports these innovations.

Basic concepts and applications of AI and ML

Artificial intelligence (AI) and machine learning (ML) are areas of computer science concerned with the development of systems capable of performing tasks that require human intelligence. These technologies have the potential to transform many aspects of our lives, from the way we work to our understanding of health and medicine. To understand the foundations and applications of these disciplines, it is helpful to familiarise yourself with some of their core concepts and typical areas of application.

Basic concepts of AI

Artificial intelligence refers to the broad field that enables machines to perform tasks that typically require human intelligence. This includes problem solving, understanding natural language, recognising patterns and images, decision making and more. AI can be divided into two main categories:

- Weak AI, also known as "applied AI", is inherent in systems designed for specific tasks, such as voice-controlled assistants or recommendation systems.
- Strong AI or "General Artificial Intelligence" refers to systems or machines that can comprehensively replicate the cognitive functioning of humans. Such systems are theoretically able to fulfil any mental task that a human user can.

Weak AI

The term "weak AI", often referred to as "applied AI", plays a central role in understanding the different types of artificial intelligence and their applications. Weak AI refers to systems that are specifically designed to fulfil a particular task or a narrowly defined set of tasks without replicating or understanding human intelligence in its entirety. This type of AI works under a fixed set of rules or learns from data to achieve specific, pre-defined goals.

A good example of weak AI are voice-controlled assistants such as Siri, Alexa or Google Assistant. These systems are trained to understand and respond to human speech, search for information, execute simple commands or answer user queries. Although their ability to process natural language and respond to a variety of requests is impressive, they operate within a very specific framework. They are not able to act outside of their programmed knowledge and capabilities or demonstrate true understanding or awareness.

Another example is recommendation systems, such as those used by streaming services like Netflix or e-commerce platforms like Amazon. These systems analyse the behaviour and preferences of users in order to make personalised suggestions for films, TV series or products. While these systems are able to provide amazingly precise recommendations based on huge amounts of data, their intelligence is limited to this specific context.

Weak AI systems are usually characterised by machine learning and data analysis. They use large amounts of data and algorithms to recognise patterns and make decisions within their area of application. Their development requires in-depth knowledge of data science and machine learning, as well as careful planning of application areas to ensure that the systems operate effectively and ethically.

Despite the limited capabilities of weak AI, its development is having a significant impact on many industries and everyday applications. It enables automation and efficiency gains in areas such as customer service, marketing, healthcare, financial services and more. Advances in weak AI are leading to ever more intelligent systems that can fulfil specific tasks with increasing precision and usefulness.

Strong AI

Strong AI, also known as Artificial General Intelligence (AGI), represents the ambitious goal of AI research to develop systems or machines that can mimic the full range of human cognitive abilities. In contrast to weak AI, which is designed for specific tasks, strong AI aims to create a universal intelligence that learns, understands, infers and is creative across a wide range of domains.

A system with strong AI would be able to fulfil any mental task that a human being can do. This includes not only specialised tasks such as playing a game of chess or diagnosing an illness, but also the ability to learn from experience, adapt to new and unknown circumstances, solve problems independently, think creatively and even possess emotions and consciousness. The realisation of such intelligence would radically push the boundaries of what machines can do and could theoretically produce machines that not only compete with humans in specific tasks, but are also able to surpass human capabilities and create independent innovations.

However, the development of strong AI raises considerable technical, philosophical and ethical questions.

From a technical perspective, research faces the challenge of developing algorithms that enable such flexible and adaptive intelligence. This could require breakthroughs in areas such as machine learning, neural networks and cognitive modelling. Philosophically, the idea of a machine possessing human-like intelligence raises questions about the nature of consciousness and identity.

Ethical considerations also play a crucial role. The possibility of machines making decisions that traditionally required human judgement raises questions about responsibility, safety and the social impact.

Although the realisation of strong AI is a fascinating vision, it remains largely speculative at this stage and a long-term prospect in research and development. Most of today's AI systems fall into the weak AI category, although advances in machine learning and AI research are constantly and rapidly pushing the boundaries of what is technologically possible. However, the move towards strong AI would not only represent a major advance in computer technology, but would also have a major impact on almost every aspect of human society.

Basic concepts of machine learning

Machine learning is a subfield of AI that uses algorithms and statistical models to enable computer programmes to learn from data and improve without being explicitly programmed. ML models learn from experience (data) to make predictions or decisions based on new, never-before-seen data. The main categories of machine learning are:

- Supervised learning, where models are trained using input-output pairs. The system attempts to learn a function that maps inputs to outputs.
- Unsupervised learning, in which algorithms learn on data sets without predefined answers and discover hidden structures in the data.
- Reinforcement learning is based on the principle of reward and punishment. An agent learns how it should behave in an environment in order to achieve the maximum reward.

Supervised learning

Supervised learning is one of the central techniques in the field of machine learning and plays a crucial role in the development of artificial intelligence.

In this method, the model is trained with a data set consisting of input-output pairs. Each pair in the training dataset consists of an input (often called a "feature") and an associated output or target (also called a "label"). The goal of supervised learning is to learn a function that represents the relationship between the input data and the output data as accurately as possible. Once the model has been trained, it should be able to predict or classify the output for new, unknown inputs.

The process of supervised learning comprises several steps. First, an algorithm is selected that appears suitable for the specific task. This could be a simple algorithm such as linear regression for continuous predictions (e.g.

predicting the price of a commodity based on its features) or a more complex one such as a deep neural network for classification tasks (e.g. recognising objects in images). The algorithm is then fed with a training dataset that helps it to "learn" the relationship between the inputs and the desired outputs.

Training a model as part of supervised learning typically involves minimising an error or loss that measures the difference between the outputs predicted by the model and the actual outputs in the training dataset. Through the training process, the model adjusts its internal parameters to minimise this error. Once training is complete, the model is evaluated against a separate dataset that it did not see during training (the test dataset) to verify its accuracy and performance.

Supervised learning is used in a wide range of applications, from speech recognition and text classification to image recognition and the prediction of stock market movements. The effectiveness of supervised learning depends heavily on the quality and quantity of the available training data. High-quality, well-annotated data enables the model to make more accurate predictions. However, collecting and labelling such data can be time-consuming and costly, which poses a challenge.

Despite this challenge, supervised learning remains a powerful method in the AI toolkit, making it possible to solve complex problems and gain valuable insights from data. The continuous improvement of algorithms, together with the increasing availability of big data and more powerful computing resources, is driving the progress and proliferation of supervised learning methods.

Unsupervised learning

Unsupervised learning is a method of machine learning that is characterised by the fact that it operates without explicitly specified answers or labels in the training data. In contrast to supervised learning, in which models are trained using examples with known input-output pairs, unsupervised learning aims to discover hidden patterns, structures or relationships within a data set that consists only of input data, without assigned outputs or labels.

This method is particularly useful in scenarios where the relationships between data points are not known in advance or when it is impossible or impractical to create a large labelled dataset. Unsupervised learning can be categorised into different techniques, including clustering, dimensionality reduction and association rule learning.

- Clustering is one of the best-known unsupervised learning techniques. Here, data points are categorised into groups (clusters) so that points within a cluster are more similar to each other than to points in other clusters. This method is often used to segment data, for example in customer segmentation in marketing, to identify groups of customers with similar preferences or behaviour.

- Dimensionality reduction is another important technique that is used to reduce the complexity of data by reducing the number of variables while trying to preserve the essential information. Techniques such as principal component analysis (PCA) are used to reduce the dimensionality of data sets, which not only saves storage space and computing time, but also helps to better understand the underlying structures of the data.
- Association rule learning is a method that aims to find interesting relationships between variables in large databases. A classic example is the "shopping basket analysis" in retail, which examines which products are frequently bought together in order to optimise sales strategies.

The challenge with unsupervised learning is that without predetermined answers, the evaluation of model performance is less clear than with supervised learning. There is no simple "right" answer, and the quality of the results often needs to be judged based on context or human expertise. Nevertheless, unsupervised learning provides powerful tools to gain insights into data that would otherwise remain hidden, especially in the early stages of data exploration when it is not yet clear what questions should be asked or what structures exist.

With the ability to recognise hidden patterns in data without relying on prior annotation, unsupervised learning is playing an increasingly important role in many areas of data analytics, from discovering new scientific insights to improving business processes and customer experiences.

Reinforcement learning

Reinforcement learning is another dynamic method of machine learning that is based on the principles of reward and punishment. At the core of reinforcement learning is an agent that learns to select the best possible actions through interaction with its environment in order to achieve its goals. This learning paradigm is inspired by behaviourist psychology and mimics the way in which living beings learn by seeking rewards and avoiding punishments.

The basic concept of reinforcement learning revolves around the agent, the environment, and how these two interact. The agent makes decisions or performs actions in each state of the environment. In response, the environment changes its state and gives feedback to the agent in the form of rewards or punishments. The reward is a numerical value that signals to the agent how favourable a particular action was. The goal of the agent is to learn a strategy (also known as a policy) that maximises the cumulative reward over time.

Reinforcement learning has found impressive applications in various fields, from the optimisation of chess and Go game strategies, where programs such as AlphaGo have reached historic milestones, to robotics, where it is used to teach robots to autonomously master complex tasks such as walking, grasping or flying. It is also used in automation and in the optimisation of decision-making processes in complex systems such as smart grids and finance.

One of the main challenges in reinforcement learning is the balance between exploration and exploitation. Exploration refers to trying out new actions to learn more about the environment, while exploitation is the use of previously acquired knowledge to maximise reward. An effective agent must learn when it is better to explore new strategies and when it is appropriate to perform proven actions.

Another challenge is scaling: many real-world problems offer an enormous or even infinite number of states and actions, which makes them difficult to solve using traditional methods. This is where advanced techniques such as deep neural networks, known as "deep reinforcement learning", come into play. These methods have the ability to learn from complex and high-dimensional data and have led to significant breakthroughs in the application of reinforcement learning.

Computing capacities for AI algorithms

The need for powerful computing capacities for the development and application of artificial intelligence cannot be emphasised enough. This dependency stems from the inherent complexity of AI algorithms, especially those that fall under the domain of machine learning (ML) and deep learning. Processing huge amounts of data, training extensive neural networks and analysing information in real time requires exceptional computing power. The reasons for these requirements can be summarised as follows:

Extensive data sets

AI and ML models learn and improve by analysing large data sets. Processing and analysing this data requires considerable computing resources. The larger the data set, the more accurately the model can recognise patterns and make predictions. However, processing such data sets in an acceptable amount of time requires high-performance computing systems.

Complexity of the models

Modern AI models, especially deep neural networks, consist of millions or even billions of parameters that need to be adjusted in order to make precise predictions or analyses. Training these models requires an immense amount of matrix multiplications and other computationally intensive operations that would be impractical without powerful hardware.

Real-time requirements

Many AI applications, such as autonomous vehicles, personal assistants and real-time translation services, require fast decision-making and responsiveness. These real-time requirements can only be met with powerful computing capacity to minimise latency and ensure a smooth user experience.

Iterative training and optimisation

The development of AI models is an iterative process in which models are continuously adapted, tested and retrained to improve their accuracy and effectiveness. This process can be tedious without fast and efficient hardware, which affects the speed of innovation and the practical implementation of research results.

Specialised hardware

The specific requirements of AI algorithms have led to the development of specialised hardware such as GPUs (Graphics Processing Units), TPUs (Tensor Processing Units) and FPGAs (Field-Programmable Gate Arrays). These are optimised for parallel processing and other computing operations typical for AI, which significantly accelerates the training and execution of AI models.

To summarise, advances in AI are inextricably linked to advances in computing power. The availability and further development of powerful computing capacities are crucial for research into new methods in machine learning, the development of more advanced and complex models and the broad application of AI technologies in industry and everyday life. Investment in computing resources is therefore a fundamental prerequisite for progress and innovation in the field of artificial intelligence.

Types of chips used in AI

The development and application of artificial intelligence is closely linked to advances in hardware technology. Different types of chips play a crucial role in AI research and application, each with their own strengths and specific areas of use. Here is an overview of the most commonly used chips in AI: CPUs, GPUs, TPUs and FPGAs.

CPUs (Central Processing Units)

CPUs, short for Central Processing Units, have long been at the heart of modern computers and play a crucial role in information processing. They are designed to handle a wide range of tasks, from the most basic calculations to complex algorithms used in data analysis, graphic design and many other areas. Essentially, CPUs act as the brain of a computer, executing instructions from programmes through a series of arithmetic operations.

The architecture of a CPU is usually divided into several cores, whereby each core is able to process tasks in parallel. This increases the efficiency and speed of the overall system, especially for programs that are optimised for multithreading. The performance of a CPU is determined by various factors, including its clock frequency, which is measured in gigahertz (GHz), the number of cores, the size of the cache memory and the efficiency of its architecture.

Modern CPUs also include special functional units such as vector processors or integrated graphics units that are optimised for specific tasks such as rendering graphics or accelerating machine learning. This development reflects the increasing demand for multifunctional devices that can support both powerful computing operations and sophisticated graphics processing.

The evolution of CPU technology over the years has led to significant increases in performance, which in turn has enabled the development of software and applications that can perform increasingly sophisticated tasks. These advances have played a key role in shaping the modern digital world, from expanding the possibilities in the field of artificial intelligence to enabling complex scientific simulations.

Despite their central role in computing technology, the future of CPUs is being challenged by emerging technologies such as quantum computing and specialised processing units, such as graphics processing units (GPUs) and field-programmable gate arrays (FPGAs). These technologies offer significant performance advantages for certain applications and could fundamentally change the way computing power is utilised in the future.

Use of CPUs in AI

CPUs are capable of handling a wide range of tasks, especially those that require sequential processing. This makes them ideal for the early stages of software development, the implementation of algorithms that do not rely on high parallelism, and for applications where the order of operations is critical. In addition, CPUs are easily accessible due to their universal presence in computers and servers, making them a practical choice for many development and computational tasks.

Despite this versatility and accessibility, CPUs have disadvantages, especially when compared to hardware specifically designed for AI computations, such as GPUs (Graphics Processing Units) and TPUs (Tensor Processing Units). These specialised processors can perform tasks that require highly parallel computing operations much more efficiently. AI and machine learning (ML) are areas that particularly benefit from this type of parallel processing capability, as they allow large data sets to be processed and complex calculations to be performed in a much shorter time.

However, GPUs, originally designed for graphics computing, have proven particularly useful for accelerating

AI and ML workloads. This is due to their ability to perform thousands of smaller calculations simultaneously, making them ideal for the matrix and vector operations that are common in these applications. TPUs, which are even more specialised, are specifically designed to accelerate tensor computations in the context of Google's TensorFlow, a widely used machine learning framework. They offer even greater efficiency for certain AI calculations.

The limitations of CPUs in terms of highly parallel AI computations lie mainly in their architecture. While they are designed for a wide range of tasks, they cannot perform the same number of operations simultaneously as GPUs or TPUs. This leads to longer execution times for tasks that rely heavily on parallel processing, which is the case for many modern AI applications. Consequently, although CPUs play an important role in the development and execution of AI programs, especially in scenarios where specialised hardware is not required or not available, they are often complemented or replaced by GPUs or TPUs when it comes to scaling and accelerating AI computations.

GPUs (Graphics Processing Units)

GPUs, or graphics processors, have undergone a significant development that goes far beyond their original applications in graphics processing.

Originally developed to speed up the display of images and videos on screens, they have become an indispensable tool for training artificial intelligence (AI) and machine learning (ML) models. This evolution has been made possible by the unique characteristics of GPUs, in particular their highly parallel architecture.

The core strength of GPUs lies in their ability to process thousands of threads simultaneously, which makes them extremely powerful for tasks that require massive parallel processing. This feature makes them ideal for training AI and ML models that need to perform complex calculations over large data sets. Unlike CPUs, which are designed for sequential processing and have a limited number of cores for parallel tasks, GPUs can perform an immense number of operations simultaneously, dramatically reducing processing time for appropriate tasks.

The training of AI and ML models is particularly computationally intensive as it requires the repeated adjustment of parameters over large data sets to optimise the model. This process involves an enormous amount of matrix and vector operations, tasks for which GPUs are particularly well suited. By using GPUs, researchers and developers can reduce the time it takes to train models from weeks or months to days or even hours, creating a faster iteration cycle and the ability to explore more complex models.

The increasing use of GPUs in AI and ML has led to specialised hardware development that is specifically optimised for this type of computation. This includes improvements in GPU architecture specifically aimed at maximising the performance and efficiency of AI computations. In addition, the proliferation of GPUs has accelerated the growth of frameworks and libraries such as TensorFlow, PyTorch and others that simplify programming for parallel processing and democratise access to GPU resources.

The transformative role of GPUs in the world of AI and ML is a clear example of how the adaptability and power of hardware can drive the development of technologies. By providing the necessary computing power to train models, GPUs have not only accelerated research and development in these fields, but also opened up new opportunities for innovation and applications that previously seemed out of reach.

GPUs are particularly effective for operations that are common in machine learning and deep learning, such as matrix multiplications. Their ability to run thousands of threads simultaneously makes them a favoured choice for training complex neural networks.

The significant acceleration that GPUs offer over CPUs in parallel processing tasks has made them an indispensable tool in the field of AI model training. This acceleration is due to the fundamental architectural differences between the two types of processors. While CPUs are designed for a wide range of tasks and are capable of executing complex instructions with a relatively small number of cores, GPUs are specifically designed to process many parallel threads. This allows GPUs to perform thousands of operations simultaneously compared to the limited parallel operations that a CPU can perform.

This ability for massive parallel processing makes GPUs particularly suitable for the training of AI models, which requires computationally intensive operations on large data sets. When training AI and ML models, millions or even billions of parameter adjustments often need to be made to improve the accuracy of the model. Each of these steps requires complex calculations that are distributed across the entire data set. The parallel processing capacity of GPUs makes it possible to perform these calculations simultaneously, which significantly reduces the time required to train a model.

In addition, developments in GPU technology and the optimisation of software and frameworks for machine learning have made GPUs even more efficient at performing these specialised tasks. Developers and researchers now have access to libraries and frameworks such as CUDA (a parallel computing platform and programming model developed by NVIDIA), TensorFlow and PyTorch, which are specifically designed to accelerate computation on GPUs. These tools provide a level of abstraction that makes it possible to effectively utilise the complex parallel processing capabilities of GPUs without the need for in-depth knowledge of the hardware.

The importance of GPUs for training AI models is also reflected in the rapid development of specialised hardware for AI computations. Companies such as NVIDIA and AMD are constantly developing new GPU models specifically designed for machine learning and AI optimisation to meet the demands of modern AI research and development. These developments not only include improvements in computing power, but also in energy efficiency, which is crucial for training increasingly complex models.

The combination of advanced hardware, specialised software and the growing availability of AI training data has ushered in an era where the boundaries of what is possible with machine learning are constantly being pushed. GPUs are a key building block enabling these advances by providing the necessary computing power to train complex models in feasible timeframes. This has not only accelerated development in traditional areas of AI, but has also enabled innovative applications in areas such as genomics, climate modelling and pattern recognition in large amounts of data.

TPUs (Tensor Processing Units)

Tensor Processing Units (TPUs) are a type of Application Specific Integrated Circuits (ASICs) developed by Google specifically to accelerate machine learning (ML) and artificial intelligence (AI) applications.

These chips represent a significant advance in hardware technology aimed at significantly improving the efficiency and speed of ML model training and inference.

TPUs are a prime example of the development of specialised hardware designed to meet the specific requirements of AI computation.

One of the key features of TPUs is their ability to perform a large number of calculations in parallel, which makes them particularly efficient for processing tensor operations. Tensors are multidimensional data arrays that play a central role in machine learning algorithms, especially in deep neural networks. By optimising for this type of computation, TPUs can train and execute ML models faster than general GPUs and CPUs, especially for applications based on Google's TensorFlow framework, which has been specifically adapted for the efficient use of TPUs.

The architecture of a TPU is designed to achieve high throughput rates for ML operations with low energy consumption. This efficiency makes TPUs particularly attractive for use in data centres and cloud computing environments, where they form the backbone of Google's ML infrastructure. TPUs make it possible to train and infer complex models faster, which accelerates the development and implementation of AI applications.

Another advantage of TPUs is their ability to work with precision-reduced data, which means that they can perform calculations with a lower numerical accuracy without significant impact on the performance or accuracy of the final model. This capability reduces memory requirements and computational load, resulting in faster calculations and more efficient utilisation of hardware resources.

Since their introduction, Google has developed several generations of TPUs, each with improvements in speed, efficiency and functionality. These developments reflect the growing importance of specialised hardware for AI applications and underline the technology industry's investment in the research and development of solutions that continue to push the boundaries of what is possible with AI.

In practice, TPUs are used in a wide range of applications, from speech processing and image recognition to recommendation systems and advanced analytical tools. Their introduction has led to significant improvements in the efficiency and accessibility of AI technologies by providing companies and developers with powerful tools to develop and implement innovative solutions.

Tensor Processing Units (TPUs) are known for their exceptional ability to quickly and efficiently perform tensor operations that are central to deep learning and machine learning. These specialised chips are designed to provide high throughput with low latency, making them particularly advantageous for the application of trained models (inference) and the training of deep learning models. Their optimisation for tensor operations enables TPUs to perform calculations common in deep learning algorithms faster than conventional processors such as CPUs and GPUs. This has a significant impact on the efficiency and speed of AI applications and services.

One of the main advantages of TPUs in the inference phase is their ability to minimise response times. This is particularly important for interactive applications where fast response times are critical to the user experience, such as in speech recognition, image recognition and real-time translation services. The low latency of TPUs makes it possible to apply complex models in real time, significantly improving the performance and responsiveness of services such as Google Search, Gmail and Google Photos.

TPUs also offer sustainable advantages when training deep learning models. Their architecture makes it possible to process a large amount of data in parallel, which significantly reduces the time needed to train models. This is invaluable in a field characterised by rapid innovation cycles and the need to constantly train larger and more complex models. The ability of TPUs to work efficiently with precision-reduced data further helps to optimise computational resources and enables researchers and developers to iterate and scale experimental approaches faster.

Another important advantage of TPUs is their energy efficiency. When processing large data sets or training complex models, energy costs can be high. TPUs are designed to provide higher computing power with lower energy consumption, which not only lowers costs but also reduces the environmental footprint of data centres.

This efficiency makes TPUs particularly attractive for use in cloud computing environments, where resources and energy consumption need to be carefully managed.

Overall, TPUs have become a critical factor in Google's infrastructure, enabling AI services and applications to accelerate and scale in ways that would not be possible with traditional hardware. Their development reflects the growing importance of specialised hardware for AI research and application and underlines the need to optimise computing resources to push the boundaries of what is possible with technology.

FPGAs (Field-Programmable Gate Arrays)

Field-Programmable Gate Arrays (FPGAs) are a special type of integrated circuits that offer a flexible and powerful solution for a variety of applications.

Unlike traditional integrated circuits, which are designed with a fixed function during manufacture, FPGAs can be configured by the end user or designer after manufacture. This flexibility allows FPGAs to be customised for specific applications or tasks, making them a versatile tool in electronics and computer engineering.

The programmable nature of FPGAs is based on a matrix of logic blocks and a variety of reconfigurable connections that allow complex digital circuits to be created. Users can customise these logic blocks and connections by loading a configuration file (often referred to as a bitstream) to realise virtually any desired logic function or digital circuit. This flexibility makes FPGAs particularly attractive for prototyping, as they allow developers to quickly iterate and customise designs without having to manufacture new hardware.

Another advantage of FPGAs is their parallel processing capability, which makes them suitable for applications that require high processing speeds, such as signal processing, cryptography and even certain types of machine learning and data processing tasks. Unlike CPUs, which process instructions sequentially, FPGAs can perform multiple calculations simultaneously, which can significantly speed up certain processes.

In addition, FPGAs offer advantages in terms of energy efficiency and latency. Since FPGAs can be configured specifically for a task, it is possible to create very efficient designs that consume less energy than general processors for the same task. Similarly, the direct implementation of algorithms at the hardware level can reduce latency, which can be critical when processing data in real-time applications.

Despite these advantages, FPGAs also have disadvantages, such as the complexity of programming and the initial costs. The design and optimisation of FPGA-based systems require specialist knowledge and tools, which can increase the barriers to entry. In addition, the initial hardware costs for FPGAs are higher compared to mass-produced chips, which can make them less attractive for end-user products.

In recent years, however, FPGAs have gained popularity, particularly in telecommunications, automotive, defence and aerospace, as well as in data centres and in accelerating cloud computing services. Their customisability and performance make them an important tool for designers and engineers working at the forefront of technology development.

The high flexibility and adaptability of FPGAs make them an attractive option for customised AI applications, especially in scenarios where processing requirements need to be precisely tailored. This ability to fine-tune to specific tasks offers significant advantages in terms of the efficiency and performance of AI systems, especially when compared to more generalised computing solutions such as GPUs and TPUs.

One of the main advantages of FPGAs in AI applications is their energy efficiency. FPGAs can be configured to perform only the necessary operations for a given task, without the overheads typical of generalised processors. This direct customisation to the task enables FPGAs to be highly energy efficient, which can be crucial in power-constrained environments or in applications where energy consumption is a critical factor. In addition, the ability to implement algorithms directly at the hardware level enables a further reduction in power consumption and improvement in overall performance.

The customisability of FPGAs is another advantage. Developers can program FPGAs for the exact needs of their AI applications, which means they can be optimised for specific tasks, such as training neural networks or performing inference. This specialisation can make FPGAs more efficient in certain use cases than GPUs or TPUs, which are optimised for parallel processing tasks but may not achieve the same efficiency for specific AI operations.

Another important aspect is the ability of FPGAs to be dynamically reconfigured to support different tasks without the need for physical intervention or hardware replacement. This flexibility allows the same FPGA resource to be used for a wide range of tasks, amortising investment costs and increasing the versatility of the hardware.

In certain scenarios, FPGAs can also offer advantages in terms of latency. As they can be optimised for specific algorithms, they enable potentially faster processing times compared to GPUs and TPUs, especially in applications that require real-time data processing.

Despite these benefits, there are challenges to using FPGAs, including the complexity of programming and the need for specialised knowledge to exploit their full capabilities. Nevertheless, for applications that require high energy efficiency, specific processing requirements or the flexibility to dynamically adapt to different tasks, FPGAs offer a powerful and adaptable solution that makes them a valuable resource in the AI hardware landscape.

The evolution of modern chips for AI applications

The evolution of modern chips for artificial intelligence marks a remarkable period in the history of computer technology, characterised by constant adaptation to the growing demands and complexities of AI applications. This evolution reflects the transition from the use of general-purpose computing units, such as CPUs, to a diverse range of specialised processors, each tailored to specific aspects of AI computation. This specialisation is a response to the exponentially increasing volumes of data and the increasing complexity of the computations required for advanced AI models.

History of hardware development specifically for AI applications.

The history of hardware development specifically for AI applications is closely interwoven with advances in artificial intelligence itself. This development history not only reflects technological progress, but also the growing need for specialised hardware to meet the increasingly demanding requirements of AI systems.

In the early days of AI research in the 1950s and 1960s, the focus was mainly on theoretical and algorithmic foundations, with the available hardware largely limited to general-purpose computers. These early computers were severely limited in their computing capacity and were not specifically designed for AI tasks. Despite these limitations, researchers such as Alan Turing and John McCarthy laid the groundwork for what AI could become, sparking discussions about machine intelligence and the potential for computers to simulate human-like intelligence.

However, the real turning point in the development of AI-specific hardware came much later, with the advent of graphics processing units (GPUs) in the 1990s. Although GPUs were originally developed to accelerate graphics applications in video games and visual media, researchers soon discovered their ability to efficiently perform parallel data processing tasks. This discovery was particularly relevant to machine learning and deep learning, areas of AI that benefit from the ability to process large amounts of data simultaneously.

With the release of CUDA (Compute Unified Device Architecture) by NVIDIA in 2007, it became easier for researchers to utilise the parallel processing capacity of GPUs for general-purpose computing (GPGPU - General-Purpose computing on Graphics Processing Units). This paved the way for the mass adoption of GPUs in AI research, as they significantly accelerated the training of deep neural networks, the basis of many modern AI systems.

Google introduced the next generation of specialised AI hardware with the development of Tensor Processing

Units (TPUs), which were unveiled to the public in 2016. TPUs were designed from the ground up for highly efficient tensor operations, which are essential for machine learning and deep learning. Their introduction marked a significant advance in the ability to train and utilise complex AI models faster and more energy efficiently.

In parallel, field-programmable gate arrays (FPGAs) have established themselves as a flexible alternative for customised AI applications. Their reconfigurability allows developers to optimise the hardware for specific AI tasks, making FPGAs particularly valuable for applications where standard GPUs or TPUs are not optimal.

Recent developments in AI hardware aim to provide even more specialised and efficient solutions for AI computation. These include neuromorphic chips, which attempt to replicate the neural structure of the human brain to further increase energy efficiency and computing power, and quantum computers, which have the potential to revolutionise the landscape of AI through their ability to solve complex problems at previously unimaginable speeds.

This ongoing evolution of AI hardware not only emphasises technological progress, but also the constant pursuit of more efficient, powerful and adaptable computing systems to push the boundaries of what is possible with AI and open up new horizons in the research and application of artificial intelligence.

Specialisation and optimisation: From GPUs to TPUs and beyond.

The evolution of artificial intelligence hardware is characterised by a continuous trend towards specialisation and optimisation, ranging from the development and proliferation of GPUs to TPUs and beyond. This movement reflects the drive to create hardware solutions that not only handle the growing demands of AI workloads, but also maximise the efficiency and performance of these systems.

The story begins with the realisation that graphics processing units (GPUs) are exceptionally well suited for machine learning and in particular for training deep neural networks due to their parallel processing capability. GPUs, which were originally developed for graphics-intensive applications such as video games, enable the simultaneous execution of thousands of calculations. This capability has proven to be crucial for accelerating AI operations that involve similarly parallelisable calculations

The emergence of tensor processing units (TPUs) has taken the specialisation of AI hardware to the next level. Developed by Google and first introduced in 2016, TPUs are specifically optimised for accelerating AI and machine learning workloads. Unlike GPUs, which are designed for a wide range of parallel computations, TPUs focus on the efficient execution of tensor operations, which are prevalent in deep learning. These highly specialised chips offer advantages in terms of throughput and energy efficiency for specific AI tasks, especially in the training and inference of AI models.

The path of specialisation and optimisation does not stop with TPUs. The industry continues to explore new architectures and technologies that can handle the challenges of AI workloads even more efficiently. These include neuromorphic chips that mimic the way the human brain works to enable even more efficient processing of AI tasks, and quantum computers that have the potential to solve certain types of problems that are inaccessible to traditional and even today's most advanced computers.

Neuromorphic chips seek to replicate the efficiency and adaptivity of neural networks in the human brain at the hardware level and could herald a new era of energy efficiency and computing power for AI applications. Quantum computers, although still at a relatively early stage of development, could achieve revolutionary breakthroughs in certain tasks such as optimisation and materials science.

These developments underline an ongoing quest in AI technology: the search for ever more specialised and optimised hardware capable of efficiently meeting the complex and data-intensive requirements of modern AI systems. While GPUs and TPUs represent significant milestones along the way, the continued innovation in this area points to a future where AI hardware will become increasingly diversified and customised to meet the specific needs and challenges posed by the next generation of AI algorithms and applications.

Although the integration of artificial intelligence (AI) in smartphones brings numerous advantages and innovative applications, developers and users alike face various challenges and limitations. These relate to technical aspects as well as questions of ethics, security and user acceptance.

Case studies: AI on smartphones and the associated chips

The integration of artificial intelligence into smartphones has resulted in a large number of applications that improve the user experience in innovative ways. Here are a few examples (more detailed in the chapter "Smartphones as a platform for AI applications"):

- Photography and image processing: Modern smartphones use AI to revolutionise photography.
- Personal assistants: Voice-controlled personal assistants such as Siri, Google Assistant and Alexa have fundamentally changed the way people interact with their smartphones.
- Health monitoring: AI-supported health applications on smartphones use sensors and data analysis to provide insights into the user's physical condition.

- Security functions: AI also improves security on smartphones, particularly through biometric authentication methods such as facial recognition and fingerprint scanners.
- Personalised recommendations and content: AI is used to learn user preferences and offer personalised content such as news, music or video recommendations. Analysing the underlying chips and hardware that enable these applications.

The AI applications in smartphones are enabled by advanced hardware and chip technology designed specifically for the efficient execution of AI and machine learning algorithms. These technologies include specialised processors, AI chips and sensors that work together to deliver the computing power, energy efficiency and functionality required for modern smartphone applications.

Specialised processors

Modern smartphones contain powerful main processors (CPUs), which are designed for general computing tasks, and graphics processing units (GPUs), which are particularly well suited for AI calculations due to their parallel processing capabilities. These processors can perform a large number of operations simultaneously, making them ideal for processing complex AI models.

Dedicated AI chips

The integration of dedicated AI chips or Neural Processing Units (NPUs) into smartphones is a significant advancement in mobile technology that is fundamentally changing the way devices process AI-related tasks. These specialised chips are designed to efficiently run machine learning and deep learning algorithms directly on the smartphone, without the need for a constant connection to the cloud. This development makes it possible to run AI applications such as speech and image recognition, real-time translation, augmented reality (AR) and much more directly on the device.

The advantages of dedicated AI chips are:

- Accelerated performance: By optimising for AI calculations, dedicated AI chips can perform tasks such as image recognition, speech processing and other AI applications much faster than conventional processors. This leads to a noticeable acceleration of applications that utilise AI functions and improves the user experience through faster response times.
- Improved energy efficiency: AI chips are not only faster, but also more energy-efficient when performing AI tasks. By minimising the energy required for AI calculations, they help to extend the battery life of devices. This is particularly important for energy-intensive applications such as

continuous voice assistants or advanced camera functions.
- Data protection: The ability to process AI-related tasks directly on the device minimises the need to send personal data to external servers or the cloud for processing. This reduces privacy concerns and increases the security of user data, as sensitive information does not have to leave the device.

Examples of AI chips in smartphones

Apple's Neural Engine

Apple's Neural Engine is an integral part of the A-series chips found in iPhones and other Apple devices. This specialised AI hardware is designed to dramatically improve the efficiency and performance of machine learning operations on the device. By integrating the Neural Engine into the A-Series chips, Apple is able to offer advanced features that utilise deep learning and artificial intelligence directly on the smartphone without relying on external servers.

Functions and applications:

- Facial recognition through Face ID: Perhaps the best-known application of the Neural Engine is Apple's Face ID technology, which enables secure biometric authentication. Face ID utilises a detailed depth map of the user's face created by machine learning to ensure secure and accurate facial recognition. This technology allows users to unlock their device, authorise payments and access sensitive applications simply by looking into the camera. The Neural Engine processes this data with high speed and efficiency to ensure a seamless user experience.

- Animated emojis (Animojis): Another highlight is the ability to create and use Animojis. Animojis are animated emojis that capture and mimic the user's facial expressions in real time. The Neural Engine analyses more than 50 different muscles in the user's face to animate emojis that reflect laughter, frowns, nods and other facial expressions in real time. This feature utilises the Neural Engine's advanced machine learning capabilities to enable a new form of digital expression.
- Improved camera functions: The camera functions of iPhones have undergone lasting improvements by utilising the Neural Engine. The engine supports advanced image processing features such as Portrait Mode, which creates a depth of field effect by focusing on the subject while blurring the background. It also enables features such as Smart HDR, which merges multiple photos into a single image with optimised dynamic range and detail. These processes require intensive AI calculations, which can be carried out efficiently on the device thanks to the Neural Engine.

The integration of the Neural Engine into the A-Series chips means that AI processing tasks can be performed locally on the device and at exceptional speed. This offers several benefits, including improved privacy and security as data does not need to be sent to external servers. In addition, efficient processing results in longer battery life and faster overall device performance. With each new generation of A-Series chips and their integrated Neural Engine, Apple is setting new standards in smartphone technology by further expanding the possibilities of machine learning and artificial intelligence.

Google's Tensor Processing Unit (TPU)

Google's use of the Tensor Processing Unit (TPU) in Pixel smartphones is a striking example of how dedicated AI hardware can improve the functionality and user experience of mobile devices. Originally developed for use in data centres to boost the performance of machine learning and AI applications, Google has adapted TPU technology to integrate it into its Pixel smartphones. This adaptation enables the devices to run sophisticated AI and machine learning processes directly on the device without the need for a constant connection to cloud-based computing resources.

- Improved camera functions: One of the outstanding features of Pixel smartphones is their camera. The integration of the TPU makes it possible to run advanced image processing algorithms directly on the device. This leads to features such as Night Sight mode, which enables impressive low-light shots without flash by utilising AI-driven algorithms to improve image brightness and quality. Other camera features that benefit from the TPU include Portrait Mode, which creates a bokeh effect by focusing on the subject and blurring the background, and HDR+, which improves the dynamic range and detail of photos.

- Voice processing: The TPU also improves the voice processing capabilities of Pixel smartphones. This includes voice recognition, which is critical for features like the Google Assistant, as well as the ability to process voice commands quickly and accurately. On-device processing enables faster Assistant response time and increases privacy by reducing the amount of data that needs to be sent to the cloud for processing.
- Personalised user experience: In addition, the TPU enables personalised user experiences by adapting and optimising the device based on the user's behaviour and preferences. This can range from customising notifications and suggestions to optimising battery life by learning which apps and services are used most frequently and how best to save energy.
- Data protection and security: A major advantage of processing AI tasks directly on the device is the improvement in data protection and security.

By processing and storing personal data such as photos, voice recordings and user behaviour on the device, the risk that this sensitive information could be compromised is reduced.

The integration of the Tensor Processing Unit in Pixel smartphones shows how dedicated AI chips can not only improve the performance and efficiency of mobile devices, but also enable completely new functions and applications that enrich the user experience. With its Pixel smartphones, Google is setting a standard for the use of AI in mobile devices by combining powerful hardware with innovative software to achieve impressive results.

Huawei's Kirin chipset with NPU

By integrating dedicated Neural Processing Units (NPUs) into its Kirin chipsets, Huawei has established itself as a pioneer in the use of specialised AI hardware in smartphones.

This strategic decision enables Huawei devices to perform sophisticated AI-based tasks directly on the smartphone with an efficiency and speed that was previously not possible. By optimising the Kirin chipsets for AI applications, Huawei offers users improved features and overall better performance, especially in the areas of camera, voice translation and power management.

- AI-controlled camera functions: One of the most notable benefits of the NPU in Huawei's Kirin chipsets is the enhancement of camera functions. Scene recognition, enabled by machine learning, can identify different objects and scenarios - such as landscapes, portraits, animals or food - and automatically adjust camera settings to achieve the best possible shot. This includes adjustments such as exposure, saturation and even the application of specific filters to visually enhance the photo. The ability to adjust settings in real time based on what the camera "sees" is revolutionising mobile photography, allowing even amateur photographers to take professional-looking photos.
- Real-time language translations: The NPU also contributes to the ability of Huawei devices to perform real-time language translations. This feature is particularly useful for travellers and business people who need to communicate in foreign countries without knowing the language. On-device processing not only ensures fast and smooth translation, but also improves privacy as the voice data does not need to be sent to external servers.
- Optimisation of energy consumption: Another major advantage of integrating an NPU into the Kirin chipset is the optimisation of energy consumption. AI algorithms can learn user behaviour and predict which apps and functions are

used most frequently to adapt energy management strategies. This can be done, for example, by shutting down rarely used apps or functions to extend battery life. The ability to intelligently manage energy consumption is particularly important at a time when screen time and mobile data usage are steadily increasing.

Huawei's integration of a dedicated NPU into the Kirin chipsets demonstrates the company's commitment to pushing the boundaries of mobile technology and providing users with powerful AI-powered features. By localising AI processing on the device, Kirin chipsets not only improve the speed and efficiency of AI tasks, but also contribute to data security and energy efficiency. These developments underline the increasing importance of specialised AI hardware in the evolution of smartphone technology and set new standards for what is expected from mobile devices.

Overall, the integration of dedicated AI chips in smartphones is a clear signal of how AI is transforming mobile technology. Not only does it enable new and improved features that enrich the user experience, but it also addresses important concerns such as data privacy and energy efficiency. As AI technology continues to develop, future generations of smartphones are expected to integrate even more powerful and specialised AI chips, opening up new possibilities for mobile applications and services.

Sensors and other hardware components

In addition to processors and AI chips, sensors play a crucial role in enabling AI applications on smartphones. Cameras, microphones, accelerometers, gyroscopes and other sensors capture a variety of data that serves as input for AI algorithms. These sensors enable functions such as facial recognition, voice assistants, health monitoring and contextual information by continuously collecting information about the environment and the user.

Optimisations at software level

To fully exploit the performance of the hardware, smartphone manufacturers and developers are also working on software optimisations, such as machine learning frameworks and operating system integrations that are specifically tailored to the hardware. These software tools and libraries enable developers to implement and utilise AI functions efficiently by simplifying communication between the application software and the hardware.

The combination of specialised processors, dedicated AI chips, advanced sensors and software optimisations form the foundation for the advanced AI applications found in modern smartphones. These technological advances allow smartphones to take on increasingly complex tasks and provide users with a richer and more seamless experience. As the hardware continues to improve, we can expect to see even more innovative AI-based features and applications that have the potential to fundamentally change the way we interact with mobile devices.

Future trends and innovations

The future development of AI chips and their impact on smartphone technologies promises to push the boundaries of what mobile devices can do. This development is expected to be characterised by a number of trends and innovations that will not only improve performance and efficiency, but also open up new applications for AI in the mobile world.

Further development of specialised AI chips

The focus on energy-efficient, high-performance AI chips will continue as chip manufacturers strive to increase computing power while minimising energy consumption. We can expect to see increasing integration of AI chips that are even better tailored to specific AI and machine learning workloads. This development will enable smartphones to run even more complex AI models directly on the device, resulting in faster and more personalised user experiences without compromising privacy.

Improving energy efficiency

Given the limited battery in smartphones, optimising the energy efficiency of AI chips will remain a key concern. Advances in chip technology, such as the use of more advanced manufacturing processes and architectures specifically designed for low power consumption, will help to extend battery life while supporting powerful AI capabilities.

Integration of AI in all aspects of smartphone technology

The integration of AI chips in smartphones marks a turning point in the evolution of mobile technologies. This development promises not only to improve existing functions, but also to introduce completely new possibilities that could fundamentally change the user experience. AI chips provide the necessary computing power directly on the device to run complex algorithms efficiently without having to rely on a connection to external servers. This opens up a world of possibilities for smartphone manufacturers and app developers to implement innovative functions that were previously impossible to realise.

- Improved user interface and gesture control: With AI chips, smartphones can learn and adapt to the preferences and habits of their users to create a personalised and intuitive user interface. This could mean that apps and settings are automatically adjusted based on context and time of day to optimise the user experience. Similarly, AI could improve gesture control by interpreting the user's intentions more accurately, enabling smoother interaction with the device.
- Advanced security functions: AI chips strengthen the security features of smartphones

by analysing biometric data more precisely, improving the recognition accuracy of features such as facial recognition and fingerprint scanners. In addition, AI-powered security systems could recognise unusual or suspicious activity on the device and take proactive measures to prevent data breaches.

- Adaptive energy management: By analysing usage data and patterns, AI can revolutionise the energy management of smartphones. AI chips enable the device to optimise energy consumption by adapting the performance of apps and functions based on actual usage. This could mean longer battery life and more efficient charging processes, increasing users' overall satisfaction with their device.
- Improved connectivity and ecosystem integration: AI chips could also change the way smartphones interact with other devices and services. By processing data in real time, AI-powered smartphones can provide more seamless connectivity and interaction with a wide range of devices such as smart home systems, vehicles and wearables. This would not only improve the user experience within the connected ecosystem, but also open up new opportunities for automation and personalisation across device boundaries.

Edge computing and the role of the cloud

The shift of AI applications from centralised cloud servers to decentralised processing directly on end devices, known as AI at the edge or edge AI, marks a transformative development in the future implementation and use of AI technologies. This movement brings AI algorithms closer to the source of data collection - i.e. directly onto smartphones, IoT devices and other edge devices - and is driven by a combination of technological, security-related and practical factors.

One of the main drivers of this development is the significant progress in semiconductor technology, which has led to more powerful and energy-efficient processors. These processors are able to process complex AI algorithms locally on the device without the need to connect to remote cloud servers. Specialised AI chips that are integrated into modern smartphones and edge devices enable fast and efficient data processing directly at the source of the data.

Another decisive factor in the shift towards edge AI is the increasing awareness of data protection and security. By processing data directly on the device, personal information remains protected and the risk of data breaches due to the transmission of sensitive data over the internet is minimised. This strengthens users' trust in the technology and promotes its acceptance.

The reduction in latency is another significant advantage of edge AI. By eliminating the need to send data to a remote server for analysis and wait for a response, edge devices can react in real time. This is particularly critical for applications that require quick decisions, such as autonomous vehicles or medical monitoring devices.

Edge AI also improves the availability of AI applications, as the devices can function independently of an internet connection. This expands the possible uses of AI in areas with poor network coverage or in situations where a connection cannot be reliably established.

Despite these numerous advantages, developers and users still face challenges. The limited resources of edge devices in terms of computing power, memory and energy capacity are limitations that need to be overcome. In addition, managing and maintaining AI models on a variety of distributed devices requires significant effort to ensure consistency and security. Finally, optimising AI models for operation on resource-limited hardware requires special expertise and adapted development tools.

Overall, AI at the edge represents a paradigm shift that is redefining the way devices process and respond to data. This development promises to usher in an era of intelligent, autonomous and privacy-friendly applications that have the potential to fundamentally change the way we understand and interact with technology. Despite existing challenges, the benefits of edge AI are clear, and its ongoing integration into everyday devices will continue to open up new and innovative application possibilities.

New materials and production techniques

Research in the field of artificial intelligence and the associated hardware is developing rapidly and involves far more than just the optimisation of existing chip architectures. A major focus of research is the development of new materials and manufacturing techniques that have the potential to revolutionise the next generation of AI chips. These innovations aim to create chips that are not only superior in terms of processing speed and capacity, but also set new standards in terms of size and energy efficiency.

Research into new materials plays a central role in overcoming the physical limitations of silicon-based semiconductors, which have formed the basis of chip technology for decades. Materials such as graphene or molybdenum disulphide (MoS2) are in the spotlight as they have exceptional electronic, thermal and mechanical properties that make them potentially superior. These materials could form the basis for chips that are thinner, more flexible and more energy-efficient while maintaining the same performance.

In parallel to the material innovations, significant progress is also being made in production technology. The development of new methods such as 3D integration, in which several chip layers are stacked on top of each other, enables transistors to be packed much more densely. This not only leads to an increase in performance and efficiency, but also enables the production of smaller and lighter devices. In addition, the use of extreme ultraviolet lithography (EUV) promises the production of structures on an even smaller scale, enabling further miniaturisation and increased chip performance.

Another exciting area of research that is pushing the boundaries of traditional chip technology is quantum computing. Although quantum computers are still in their infancy and their direct application in everyday devices is a long way off, the basic principles of quantum computing could open up new avenues for the architecture of AI chips. Quantum bits, or qubits, offer the possibility of performing calculations in a way that is not possible with conventional bits and could one day lead to an exponential increase in processing capacity.

Despite the enormous potential of these innovations, researchers and engineers face considerable challenges. The integration of new materials and manufacturing techniques into mass production requires extensive research and development as well as investment in new production facilities and processes. In addition, issues of compatibility, reliability and cost-effectiveness must be addressed.

However, advances in the development of new materials, manufacturing techniques and theoretical models such as quantum computing point to a promising future. They could lead to AI chips that are not only more powerful and energy efficient, but also open up new form factors and application possibilities. These developments could fundamentally change the way we interact with and benefit from technology, ushering in a new era of digital innovation.

The future development of AI chips therefore promises to significantly expand the capabilities of smartphones by enabling more powerful, efficient and intelligent devices. These advances will not only improve the technical specifications of smartphones, but also open up new possibilities for the application of AI in our daily lives, continuing to change and improve the way we interact with technology.

Challenges in the further development of AI-enabled chips for smartphones

The further development of AI-enabled chips for smartphones is at the centre of technological innovation, but also poses specific challenges. These range from technical limitations to privacy concerns and sustainability issues. A discussion of these challenges sheds light on the complexity behind the scenes of the smartphone industry and offers insights into the future of mobile AI.

- Energy efficiency vs. performance: One of the biggest dilemmas in the development of AI chips for smartphones is the balance between performance and energy consumption. AI applications require significant computing power, which is in direct conflict with the goal of energy efficiency to extend battery life. The development of chips

that are both powerful and energy-efficient remains a key challenge.
- Miniaturisation: The ongoing miniaturisation of chip technologies is reaching physical limits in terms of the packing density of transistors and the associated heat dissipation. These limitations require innovative approaches in chip architecture and manufacturing processes to further increase performance without increasing device size or generating excessive heat.
- Cost: The development and production of advanced AI chips is costly. These costs can affect the price of smartphones, potentially limiting the accessibility and market penetration of advanced AI features.
- Data protection: With the increasing processing of personal data directly on the device by AI chips, concerns about data protection are also growing. Ensuring that this data is protected from unauthorised access poses a considerable challenge.
- Security: The complexity of AI chips and the algorithms running on them increase the risk of security vulnerabilities that could be exploited by malicious actors. Ensuring the security of these chips against attacks is crucial for the protection of user data and the integrity of the devices.
- Resource consumption: The production of advanced AI chips requires significant quantities of rare materials and resources, the extraction and

processing of which can raise environmental and socio-political concerns.
- Waste and recycling: With rapid technological progress and the resulting cycle of upgrades and replacements of old devices, challenges arise with regard to electronic waste and the recycling of valuable materials.

Overcoming these challenges requires a combination of continued research and development, interdisciplinary collaboration and a commitment to ethical standards and sustainability. While technological innovations can provide solutions to some of these problems, other challenges require a careful balancing process between the benefits of AI applications and the potential impact on privacy, security and the environment. The future of AI-enabled chips in smartphones will therefore be characterised not only by - almost inevitable - technological breakthroughs, but also by the industry's ability to act responsibly and in line with societal values.

We may be on the eve of significant technological breakthroughs enabled by AI. From medicine, where AI could provide more accurate diagnoses and personalised treatment plans, to environmental science, where it could play a role in monitoring and combating climate change, the applications are diverse. In industry, automation through AI could lead to more efficient production processes, while in education, customised learning experiences could be created for each student.

The introduction of further AI technologies is likely to bring about significant economic and social changes. While some occupations could be replaced by automation, new jobs requiring specialised skills could emerge. This change could lead to a redistribution of the labour force and increase the need for retraining and upskilling. At the same time, AI could help to address social challenges, for example by improving access to healthcare and education.

The increasing presence of AI also raises lasting ethical and moral questions. Issues such as decision-making by algorithms, the privacy of data and the potential loss of human interaction require careful consideration. It will be necessary to develop ethical frameworks that ensure that AI is used for the benefit of all and does not lead to an increase in inequalities.

The regulation of AI will play a crucial role in finding a balanced approach between promoting innovation and protecting society from potential risks. The development of international standards and guidelines could help to maximise the positive aspects of AI while minimising undesirable consequences.

Reflection on the future of AI paints a picture full of potential and challenges. The key to success lies in a balanced approach that takes into account technological advances, ethical considerations, social values and economic conditions. Ultimately, it is our shared responsibility to shape the development and implementation of

AI technologies in such a way that they contribute to the greatest possible benefit for society as a whole.